MW00713166

A Walk Thru the Life of

PETER

Growing Bold Faith

Walk Thru the Bible

BakerBooks

a division of Baker Publishing Group
Grand Rapids, Michigan

© 2009 by Walk Thru the Bible

Published by Baker Books
a division of Baker Publishing Group
P.O. Box 6287, Grand Rapids, MI 49516-6287
www.bakerbooks.com

Printed in the United States of America

Library of Congress Cataloging-in-Publication Data
A walk thru the life of Peter : growing bold faith / Walk Thru the Bible.
      p.   cm.
   Includes bibliographical references.
   ISBN 978-0-8010-7172-0 (pbk.)
   1. Peter, the Apostle, Saint. 2. Bible. N.T.—Study and teaching. 3. Bible. N.T.—
Criticism, interpretation, etc. I. Walk Thru the Bible (Educational ministry).
BS2515.W24 2009
225.9'2—dc22   2008050827

Cover image: Donald Gruener / iStock

Contents

Introduction

Jerry has been sitting behind the same desk for the past five years, but this morning is different. No longer is he a marketing representative; today, he's the company's new vice president. He has been dreaming about this day for a long time. He's full of hope, but he's also rattled by huge doubts. Does he have what it takes to succeed in his new position? What if he fails?

Just twenty-four hours ago, Karen was listening to her pastor speak about how followers of Jesus should stand up for their faith. It inspired her so much that she resolved to be bolder. Yet during her morning break today, a couple of coworkers were making fun of Christians, and what did she do? She bit her lip and slipped out of the break room.

Part of Steve wants to be the best husband he can be, and part of him just wants to shut everyone out—especially when he's tired or has a lot on his mind. And lately that happens far too often. His desire to be a better husband gets overruled by his desire to do his own thing.

Like Jerry, Karen, and Steve, Peter, the leader of Jesus's chosen twelve, knew what it was like to struggle, to doubt, to achieve, to fail, to hit the bull's eye, and to miss the target completely. And in spite of all that, Jesus called him a "rock." He was the disciple Jesus often called upon as a spokesman for the others. The only disciple to ever say "no" to the Lord. The one who defiantly professed he would die for the Master. The disciple who, when Jesus needed support the most, blatantly denied even knowing him.

Brimming with competing strengths and weaknesses, Simon Peter had a nature much like ours. One minute, he would boldly walk on water. In the next, he would cry out in mortal fear as he sank. While wanting with all his heart to act nobly, he frequently found himself taking the easy way out. At times when he should have remained quiet, he opened his mouth and said things he instantly regretted. He was the spiritual equivalent of someone biting off more than he can chew.

If you can relate to Peter wanting to do one thing but coming up short, then there's good news. Just as Jesus never gave up on Peter, he will never give up on you. And just as Peter eventually grew to become the follower of Jesus he desperately wanted to be, God has the same plans for you.

In the course of your study of Peter's life, you'll get to know this vocal disciple better than ever. You'll gain a better idea of his strengths and weaknesses. You'll spot the obstacles that tripped him up, and you'll discover that the world Peter lived in and the issues he faced are not as far removed from us as we might think.

Like Peter, you have strengths and weaknesses. You may experience moments of peace punctuated by seasons of worries, troubles, and trials. Though you enjoy impressive triumphs in your spiritual walk, you've also been known to stub your spiritual toe, stumble, and fall. And that, apparently, is okay. It simply means you're living on the human side of glory. It also means that, like Peter, you can become exactly who God has destined you to be. And just as Peter was Jesus's friend, so are you.

Cephas

Simon was vigorous and strong. As a fisherman, he had to be. The fisherman's life was a hard and busy one, with frequent long nights of setting large nets and pulling them back in. As commercial fishing is today, so was Peter's job one of the riskiest and most deadly occupations in the world. Violent storms would frequently whip up the Sea of Galilee virtually without warning, threatening the lives of all trying to ride its ravaging waves.

Because of his unapologetic declaration of Jesus as the Messiah, Jesus called Simon "the Rock." And he fulfilled his nickname: he demonstrated both the positives and the negatives of being stubbornly unmovable. The sinful side of stubbornness would have made him an obstacle. But in the Spirit, he was a constant strength during persecution.

Peter was a family man. In fact, based on the Scriptures and the layout of what archeologists believe to be his house in Capernaum, it seems that Peter's mother-in-law, his brother Andrew, and perhaps Andrew's family lived with him and his wife. He was also a leader. Every time the disciples are listed, his name is first. And he was a man of faith—the only disciple to step out on water.

Peter's stop-and-start spirituality gave way on the day of Pentecost to bold and consistent ministry in Jerusalem and beyond. He became one of the leaders of the early church—the first to embrace the Spirit's work among Gentiles and one of the foremost apostles to the Jews. His missionary travels eventually led him to Rome where, under the emperor Nero, he would give his life for Jesus.

How to Use This Guide

The questions in this guide are geared to elicit every participant's input, regardless of his or her level of preparation. Obviously, the more group members prepare by reading the biblical text and the background information in the study guide, the more they will get out of it. But even in busy weeks that afford no preparation time, everyone will be able to participate in a meaningful way.

The discussion questions also allow your group quite a bit of latitude. Some groups prefer to briefly discuss the questions in order to cover as many as possible, while others focus only on one or two of them in order to have more in-depth conversations. Since this study is designed for flexibility, feel free to adapt it according to the personality and needs of your group.

Each session ends with a hypothetical situation that relates to the passage of the week. Discussion questions are provided, but group members may also want to consider role-playing the scenario or setting up a two-team debate over one or two of the questions. These exercises often cultivate insights that wouldn't come out of a typical discussion.

Regardless of how you use this material, the biblical text will always be the ultimate authority. Your discussions may take you to many places and cover many issues, but they will have the greatest impact when they begin and end with God's Word itself. And never forget that the Spirit who inspired the Word is in on the discussion too. May he guide it—and you—wherever he wishes.

Calling

"Meir said he and Miriam were going to hear him," Erez told his wife, Hadassah, while pulling his tunic over his head.

"When?" she asked.

Erez straightened the tunic and shrugged. "I don't know. Soon, I think."

He walked over to the table where Hadassah was making his breakfast, packing some olives inside yesterday's bread. "Do you think he could really be the one?" Erez asked, tinges of excitement and hope in his voice. He lifted dark, handsome eyes while waiting for his wife to answer.

"Erez, you know more than I about such things. Do you?"

"I don't know. I can't see where living in the wilderness like a wild man and dipping people in the water would make you a prophet."

Hadassah handed the bread to her husband and laid a hand on his shoulder. "You want to go see him, don't you?" she asked.

9

He sighed and shook his head. "When would I ever get time?" He kissed her on the forehead and left for work, eating his breakfast along the way.

Hadassah stepped to the door and watched her husband walk down the road. He was a good, hardworking man, currently employed to pave the dusty streets of Capernaum with small stones.

When Erez rounded the corner out of site, Hadassah whispered to herself, "Well . . . I've got a lot to do today." Her to-do list was longer than a camel's neck, and topping the list was a trip to the fish market for some sardines the fishermen would have caught overnight.

These days, she looked forward to her trips to the market. There was always news, and recently something very interesting had been fueling the gossip. It seemed that the same thing that had caught her husband's attention had gotten the whole town talking. Many in Capernaum had even traveled down the banks

LIVING IN A FISH BOWL

Imagine living less than one hundred feet from the only church in town, and instead of cars zooming past your house, chattering people—people who know who you are—amble slowly by your front door on their way to worship? Would you feel as though you were living in a fish bowl?

Archeologists believe they have found Peter's house, and it's only a stone's throw from the Capernaum synagogue where Jesus did much of his teaching. His home eventually became a house church where believers met to worship. In the fifth century, an octagonal-shaped church was built on the site. Recent excavations of the original house have uncovered fish hooks and hundreds of graffiti markings on the walls, some of which refer to Jesus, Peter, and other early Christian figures.

of the Jordan to see the baptizer Yochannon. He was a strange, Elijah-like figure—a voice in the wilderness, attired in camel hair, living on a diet of locusts and wild honey.

Whatever he was—prophet or peculiarity—people from towns all around were flocking to hear him preach. "Repent, for the kingdom of heaven is at hand!" he would shout. Then he would immerse the repentant in the river.

Maybe today at the market there would be fresh news of this prophet. Maybe someone would know what he meant by "kingdom of heaven." And maybe—just maybe—Hadassah and Erez would soon travel to the Jordan to see for themselves.

―――⧟―――

Such might have been a common scene in Capernaum just days prior to Jesus entering the town, calling some of its young men—including Simon—to follow him. The section of the Jordan River where John the Baptist might have been preaching was not far away, and Scripture tells us that people were flocking to see him. Many of them probably wondered if the baptizer might be a long-awaited prophet or even the Messiah.

God was busy orchestrating events. The baptizer was center-stage, urging people everywhere to turn from their sins. Soon he would point people to the Messiah. And the Messiah would enter the bustling town where he spent much time with his friend Simon.

The Gaze: John 1:35–42

Andrew has been a disciple of the Baptizer. One day when he is with his teacher, Jesus comes walking by. "Behold the Lamb

PETER'S BOAT?

In 1986, after several years of drought, the water level in the Sea of Galilee dropped low enough to expose the outline of a genuine first-century fishing boat. The boat was carefully extracted and is now on display at the Nof Ginosar Kibbutz. At twenty-six feet long and seven and a half feet wide, it's easily large enough to carry several fishermen, their nets, and a nice catch of fish . . . or, perhaps, a Savior and twelve of his followers. Though the natural odds of this boat having actually belonged to Simon Peter are very slim, the discovered vessel is exactly the kind Peter and Andrew (or James and John) would have owned.

of God!" John announces (John 1:36). Andrew and another of John's disciples leave to follow Jesus.

The first thing Andrew wants to do is share the news of the Messiah. After spending the day with Jesus, his first impulse is to find his brother Simon. "We have found the Messiah," he exclaims.

The Messiah? Simon must have wondered. To his credit, he believes enough to accompany his excited brother to see Jesus. When they meet, Jesus looks at him, gazing deep into his soul. Jesus sees the real Simon—what he will become—and gives him a prophetic name: "You are Simon son of John. You will be called Cephas" (John 1:42). *Cephas*, or *kefa*, is Aramaic; it's *petros* in Greek, and *stone* in English. This disciple will be a rock.

Discuss

- Imagine Jesus gazing into your soul as he did with Peter. What obstacles might he see that could hinder you from

12

serving him the way he desires? What potential might he see in you?

_____

_____

_____

_____

- If you encountered Jesus while going about your business today, what do you think would he call you to do?

_____

_____

_____

_____

The Call: Matthew 4:18–22; Luke 5:1–11

We've seen how Andrew brought his brother, Simon, to Jesus—and how Jesus identifies his potential as a solid leader (John 1:35–42).

Matthew 4:18–22 details a second instance of Simon's call. Simon and Andrew are busy casting their nets into the Sea of Galilee when Jesus approaches. "Come, follow me," he says, "and I will make you fishers of men" (4:19). The brothers drop their nets and follow.

Some time later, before Jesus has taken his new disciples beyond Capernaum, Simon and Andrew are at work again. Luke 5:1–11 tells of Jesus preaching by the shore as crowds press in to hear him. The brothers are washing their nets as their empty boats sit nearby. Jesus asks Simon to take him out from shore so he can use the boat as a platform for teaching the crowds. Later, Jesus returns the favor—and then some. He urges Simon to launch into deep water and let down his nets.

The result? So many fish that Simon has to call for help to haul them all in.

Discuss

- Has Jesus ever been as persistent with you as he apparently was with Peter? Has he ever convinced you that his authority and your call to service are legitimate?

_____

_____

_____

_____

_____

_____

A CASE STUDY

Imagine: You're a professional bass fisherman, and it's tournament time. At the starting gun, you jump in your boat and jet down the shoreline of the lake. When you get to what looks like a good spot, you start fishing, paying close attention to factors such as location, conditions, and changes in the environment. You use various tackle throughout the day—shiny lures, plastic worms, and more—tied to the end of a strong line that's wound onto high-tech reels secured to graphite poles.

- Do you think being a "fisher of men" requires a similar level of intentionality? Why or why not?
- Do you think the calling to fish for people was specifically for Peter and the disciples or for every Christian? To what extent do you see yourself as a fisher?
- What kinds of "tackle" do you think are most effective in drawing people into God's kingdom? What have you found to be ineffective? Why?

15

Zeal

Steve, Jason, and Barry shouted at the top of their lungs as the receiver caught the ball, faked out the cornerback, and headed down the sideline. The team hadn't played this well since they were fraternity brothers together in college two decades ago.

"*Go!*" Steve screamed, hitting Jason on the back, almost knocking the popcorn out of his hand. "He's at the forty, the thirty . . ." gasped the announcer. The receiver cut back inside, leaving the last defender grasping at air. "The twenty! The ten! *Touchdown!*"

The three friends jumped and yelled as popcorn flew everywhere. It was one of the most exciting Saturday afternoons they'd had in years.

Sunday morning, as always, found Barry in church, singing his heart out: "Every knee shall bow, every tongue confess. . . ." Lowering his eyes, Barry spotted the empty seat where Steve

MOSES AND ELIJAH

Two men appeared with Jesus at the transfiguration: Moses and Elijah. There are hardly more significant names in Jewish history, but why were these two men in particular significant? First, Hebrew Scripture was often called "the Law and the Prophets." Moses is the key figure of the Law, and Elijah was considered the prototypical prophet. Together, they represented all of God's Word to Israel. The transfiguration was a graphic picture of the Word pointing to the Son.

In addition, a "return" of both had been foretold. Moses had prophesied that a prophet like him—someone as significant and influential as the one who brought deliverance, truth, and the Promised Land—would one day come. "You must *listen to him*," Moses said (Deut. 18:15). And Malachi 4:5 had prophesied a return of Elijah. On both counts, expectations were high (see John 1:21, 25, for example). The voice that thundered from heaven proved that the time of John the Baptist and Jesus was the long-awaited fulfillment of these prophecies. God's voice even echoed Moses's instructions: "Listen to him!" (Mark 9:7).

and his wife used to sit. "We haven't stopped coming," Steve would always assure his friend. "We'll be there one of these days." But that day never seemed to come.

Then Barry noticed Jason standing with his wife a couple of rows in front—very still, very silent, and very uncomfortable. Barry's nickname for Jason's typical church expression was "hymn face." He always looked like he couldn't wait for the song to end. *That's not the Jason from the football game*, Barry thought. *Why?*

Passion is a rare commodity in the lives of some Christians. Though the cosmic spectacle of Jesus's victory over evil and pain is spread open to the eyes of faith, it's still sometimes hard to see. Believers who express zeal in some aspects of life

KEYS AND THE CONFESSOR

"I will give you the keys of the kingdom." Those are Jesus's words to Peter (Matt. 16:19) after Peter identifies Jesus as the Messiah. Jesus draws a connection between the confession and the keys; recognizing who he is gives his followers a certain authority in spiritual issues. The keeper of the keys in a household was generally the head servant, a close confidant of the master of the house. In the temple, this role figuratively belonged to the high priest—the one who had a unique right of entry into the presence of God. By confessing Christ for who he is, Peter—and we—draw close to him in friendship and responsibility.

find it hard to be enthusiastic about the gospel. Whatever we can say about Peter, he doesn't fit in that category. He wears his emotions on his sleeves and speaks before he thinks. And Jesus loves him for it.

A Bold Attempt: Matthew 14:22–33

It has been a long, emotional day for both Jesus and the disciples. Soon after learning of the death of John the Baptist, Jesus and his disciples sail to a remote place. They need time alone, time to talk, pray, and reflect. But crowds follow along the shore, so while he was grieving for his friend and cousin, Jesus set aside his own needs and the needs of his devoted nucleus of twelve. They miraculously feed five thousand people. Exhausted, Jesus directs his disciples to again set sail while he sends the crowd away. Then he goes up on a mountainside alone to pray.

During the evening, the weather on the Sea of Galilee turns nasty. Wind funneling through the hills along the shore whips across the water, birthing treacherous waves. From the mountainside, Jesus could see the boat tossed by the waves before darkness fell. Now, in complete darkness, he begins walking across the water toward the boat.

The last thing anyone expects to see during a storm at sea is a person walking toward them on the water. As Jesus approaches the boat, the disciples are terrified. He calls out to them, assuring them of who he is. If so, Peter remarks, he should be able to walk on water too. Jesus invites him to try—and he does! For a moment anyway. When he sees the unlikelihood of it, he falters. Jesus tells him why—the issue was faith—and helps him up. In his zeal, Peter has done the impossible.

Discuss

- Can you think of a situation in which your zeal has gotten you "in over your head"? Did God help you in that situation?

  _____

  _____

  _____

  _____

- What did Peter experience when he kept his eyes on Jesus? What did he experience when he stared at the circumstances (wind and waves)? In your difficult times, which do you tend to gaze at—Jesus or circumstances—and why?

  _____

  _____

  _____

  _____

19

Hasty Words: Mark 9:1–10

Just six days after Peter confesses that Jesus is the Messiah (Mark 8:29), he, James, and John are allowed to witness a remarkable scene: Jesus in his glory. This inner circle of disciples is led up a mountain—perhaps the nine thousand two hundred-foot peak of Mount Hermon—where Moses and Elijah appear and discuss Jesus's impending sacrifice with him. The Messiah is transfigured into bright light, and Peter speaks. "Rabbi, it is good for us to be here. Let us put up three shelters—one for you, one for Moses and one for Elijah" (9:5). In writing the story later, Mark seems to almost apologize for Peter's blunder: "He did not know what to say, they were so frightened" (9:6). Zeal has again put Peter out on a limb. He goes down in history for treating the Son of Glory as next in line to two of Israel's greatest prophets.

Moses and Elijah exit the scene, but Jesus, of course, remains. A bright cloud envelops the foursome, and a voice thunders from heaven. This is the beloved Son. On the way down the mountain, the disciples are forbidden to disclose what they've seen. Among themselves, they try to figure out an enigmatic phrase: "rising from the dead."

Discuss

- How often do you think Christians today speak up too quickly and unwittingly about sacred mysteries we don't understand? How do you think Jesus would respond to our uninformed declarations?

    _____

    _____

    _____

Confessions: John 6:41–69; Matthew 16:13–20

Confessions are powerful. They can completely change a life. Jesus emphasized that confessing him was a high-stakes decision that would make the difference between life and death. Peter seldom shied away from saying how he felt. He wore his heart on his sleeve. In many cases, that led to verbal blunders. In others, it led to bold confessions.

After feeding five thousand people in a remote area, Jesus reminds the crowd of another feeding in the wilderness: the manna that fell from heaven. And, in fact, Jesus is the true manna, the bread sent by God from heaven. Not only that, he says that eating this bread—his body—and drinking his blood are essential for sharing his life.

These are hard words to hear, and not everyone can handle them. In fact, most can't. In the low point of his popularity after his public ministry began, the crowds abandon him. And Jesus turns to his closest disciples: "You do not want to leave too, do you?"

Peter, as always, speaks for the group. "Lord, to whom shall we go? You have the words of eternal life. We believe and know that you are the Holy One of God" (6:68–69). It's a startling confession. In a few simple words, he has affirmed that the disciples aren't following Jesus because he's popular. Neither do they follow him because they understand everything he says. No, they are in it for the long haul because Jesus has words of life. The disciples have left everything to follow him because his teaching comes from above. And in this case, Peter's words are exactly the right answer.

On another occasion, Jesus asks his disciples who the people in the villages think he is. The answers are a mixed bag that includes John the Baptist, Elijah, Jeremiah, or perhaps one of the other prophets. But the more pressing question is who his disciples, those closest to him, think he is. And, of course, the first to speak is Simon bar Jonah, the spokesman. "You are the Christ, the Son of the living God" (16:16).

This is a landmark confession and the moment most closely tied to Simon's nickname: the Rock. These words are essential for salvation; those who come to Jesus in faith must believe that he is the Messiah, the Son of the living God. Though Peter has spoken quickly, he has spoken words that come only by revelation from God.

Discuss

- How strong do you think your commitment to Jesus would be if only twelve people in your city believed in him? Why?

  _____

  _____

  _____

  _____

- Do you think it makes a difference to God whether people confess the truth out loud or simply believe the truth in their hearts? Why or why not?

  _____

  _____

  _____

  _____

A CASE STUDY

Imagine: You've lived all your life in a society that forbids any open discussion of Jesus and the Bible. You've known very few Christians, and none of them have talked with you about their beliefs because they aren't sure where you stand. You've heard of Christians who were tortured and killed for violating religious laws. And now the government wants to monitor religious discussion even more closely. Next week, everyone in the country will have to register their faith with local officials. And while Christianity is legal—for now—confessing Jesus would certainly invite harassment by anyone with access to government records. And with your life closely monitored because of your declared beliefs, any hint of a whisper of your faith outside your home could result in severe consequences.

- Would you honestly declare your faith as the government requires or continue to keep it secret to prevent suspicion?
- If you declare your faith for the record, would you abide by the laws forbidding any and all discussion of it?
- In what ways could you communicate the love of Christ to others without breaking any laws?

Denial

"Here!" Yakim said as they rounded the corner to the market. "This is where he was." For a moment, the two friends looked as far as they could down the busy street, past booths where merchants peddled grain, fruit, vegetables, and clothes.

"Well, he's not here now," Omer sighed.

"Right there," Yakim said as he pointed at the spot. "That's where he healed the blind man." Yakim put his hands on Omer's shoulders as he looked his friend square in the eyes and said. "I saw it with my own two eyes."

"All right . . . I believe you already." Omer pulled away and straightened his cloak. "But do you really have to take it this far . . . to believe what he says?"

Yakim didn't answer.

"Come on," his friend urged, "tell me about your father. He didn't *really* kick you out of the house, did he? He wouldn't

24

BEHIND THE SCENES

Peter's denial of Jesus was the product of more than disillusionment and self-preservation. There was a behind-the-scenes battle going on. "Simon, Simon," Jesus had said to him, "Satan has asked to sift you as wheat" (Luke 22:31). We don't know what Jesus's exact response to this unholy request was, other than the fact that he obviously gave permission. But there's some encouragement in this foreboding comment: in order for Peter to be so severely tested, Satan had to ask permission, and Jesus had to grant it—which means that our greatest enemy is on a leash that's held by our greatest ally. And Jesus is clearly the master of the situation. Verse 32 implies that he knows Peter will fall; that he has prayed for Peter ahead of time; and that he counts Peter's return and restoration as a fact. Peter, for his part, learned his lesson well; 1 Peter 5:8–11 seems to be written by someone who knows his subject firsthand.

do that. Not just for talking about Yeshua. What did he really say?"

"What did he say?" Yakim echoed the question. "I told you. He said, 'Out.'"

"That's it? Just 'out'?"

"He said that if Yeshua was a good man, the priests would say so and welcome him. But instead, they are talking about putting people out of the fellowship for believing him."

"Out of the synagogue? Are you sure?"

Yakim nodded. "For calling him the Messiah."

A strong hand gripped Yakim's shoulder. "What are you two boys up to?" a friendly voice spoke. He turned to see the smiling face of Lavi, one of his father's best friends—and a good friend of the ruler of the synagogue.

"We . . ." Omer began, "we're not doing anything."

"I'm surprised to see you here," Yakim said calmly.

"Part of my responsibility, Yakim. I'm keeping my eyes open for the man some poor souls are calling a prophet."

"For Yeshua?" Yakim's voice sounded weaker than he intended.

Lavi looked at Yakim inquisitively, his long robes flowing in the gentle breeze.

"I saw him do a miracle here," Yakim offered. Lavi would find out eventually from his father anyway, and perhaps his own admission would earn more respect.

"Uh...what Yakim means," Omer interjected, "I mean...." He gave up fumbling for words. "I've got to go," he said abruptly, nearly toppling a basket of fruit from a woman's arms as he left.

"Yakim, I have known your family a long time. You know that. Your father is a friend of mine. Listen to me, Yakim...."

TWO REPENTERS

Peter denied Jesus and wept bitterly because of his failure (Matt. 26:75). Judas betrayed Jesus and, seized with remorse, he acknowledged his sin, tried to return the money he had been paid for his treachery, and then hanged himself (Matt. 27:3–5). So why was Peter's repentance treated so tenderly by Jesus while Judas's remorse was condemned? Consider the differences:

Judas's sin was premeditated backstabbing; Peter's was a heat-of-the-moment stumble. Judas's betrayal was well-orchestrated; Peter's denial happened in spite of his best intentions. Judas's remorse never led to any confession to Jesus, return to the fold, or trust in God's forgiveness; Peter's sorrow prompted his undying loyalty to the mercies of God and a lifelong ministry in Jesus's name. The two portraits of sin and grief seem to illustrate a truth explained later by Paul: "Godly sorrow brings repentance that leads to salvation and leaves no regret, but worldly sorrow brings death" (2 Cor. 7:10).

Yakim braced himself.

"Go home," Lavi urged. "Don't give this lunatic a second thought. Go home."

"But I saw him. Right here. He made the beggar see."

"Yakim, I'm telling you this because I care. You're a young man now, but there are things you do not understand. Our fathers paid a dear price for ignoring the Lord's warnings. We will not do that again. I will protect our beliefs at all costs—even if it means shunning the son of a friend. Follow Omer's example. Go home and do not mention this again."

Lavi turned and continued his walk. But Yakim would not move.

———— ∞ ————

There are critical times in our lives when we either stand up for what we believe or cave in to pressure. Peter saw himself as the kind of man who stands firm, but he overestimated his commitment on at least one traumatic occasion. This close friend of Jesus denied ever having known him personally.

Though there is often a heavy price to pay for being uncompromising about our faith, the price of caving in is heavier. The good news is that even if we fail and weep bitterly about it, God doesn't give up on us. In fact, people who fail are exactly the kind of people Jesus came to redeem and restore.

Pledge: Matthew 26:17–35

The disciples had egos. In other words, they were human. And human beings get jealous, especially of those who seem to find themselves in the limelight much too often—which, of course, is exactly where Simon Peter seemed to live. So when Peter

27

declared that he would never deny Jesus, even if everyone else in the room did, he probably didn't cultivate many warm, fuzzy feelings among his peers. In fact, the implication that he was more faithful than the other disciples was likely offensive. Unintentionally offensive, of course, but offensive nonetheless. Loudmouths who don't understand subtleties of human relationships often trample unknowingly on others' feelings.

Peter could have simply said, "I will never forsake you," but he didn't. He compared himself with all other potential responses and affirmed that his would be the strongest and most faithful response among his peers. As Proverbs 16:18 says, "Pride goes before destruction, a haughty spirit before a fall." And Peter would soon land hard.

Discuss

- In 1 Peter 5:5–6, Peter quotes an Old Testament passage about God opposing the proud but giving grace to the humble. He therefore urges his readers to humble themselves under God's hand in order that they might be lifted up at the proper time. In what ways did Peter experience the realities of this passage? In what ways have you?

　　_____

　　_____

　　_____

　　_____

- How have you seen spiritual pride manifested in Christianity in general? In your church? In your life?

　　_____

　　_____

　　_____

Denial: Luke 22:54–62

Amid the confusion of Jesus's arrest and trial, Simon the Rock denies ever having known him—repeatedly. Fear of people's opinions or swords can do that; it magnifies our circumstances and our concern for immediate safety or respect, and it shrinks our view of God and eternity. It skews our perspective and makes us unwise.

Luke records a heartwrenching detail of Peter's three denials. When the rooster crowed, "the Lord turned and looked straight at Peter." The first time Jesus gazed at Peter was when they first met, when followers were gathering around this Messiah. Jesus saw Peter's potential underneath his rough exterior and called him a rock. Now, on a cold night three years later, as disciples are scattering and abandoning this Messiah, Jesus again gazes into Peter's soul. And Peter leaves and weeps bitterly.

Discuss

- If Jesus stood before you right now and gazed into your eyes, what do you think he would see? Knowing that your heart is laid completely bare before him, how would you feel about being in his presence? Why?

_____

_____

_____

_____

Restoration: Mark 16:7; 1 Corinthians 15:5; John 21:15–17

Peter's betrayal of Jesus was dramatic and devastating. Perhaps more than any other disciple besides Judas, he failed. Not only did he abandon Jesus in a crisis moment, he vocally disowned him. His confidence in his complete faithfulness had proven unfounded.

In at least three instances, Scripture provides a glimpse of God's mercy toward Peter after his failure.

The first is a small but important mention of Peter in Mark 16:7. When three women arrive at the tomb to anoint Jesus's body, an angel tells them Jesus has risen and then gives them a tender instruction: "Go, tell his disciples *and Peter*, 'He is going ahead of you into Galilee. There you will see him, just as he told you'" (emphasis added). Clearly, God had plans.

Peter is apparently the first disciple Jesus appears to after the resurrection—alone. Paul tells us in 1 Corinthians 15:5 that Jesus first met with Peter before meeting with the rest of the disciples, as though the two of them had an important matter to discuss apart from the group. And, in fact, they did.

Finally, toward the end of John's gospel, Jesus appears to the disciples on the shore of the Sea of Galilee. Three times—once for each denial—he asks Peter if he loves him. And Peter takes advantage of the opportunity to counter each of his denials with a confession of love and loyalty. He is not only forgiven but fully restored.

Discuss

- What's the difference between forgiveness and restoration? Have any of your failures caused you to doubt God's willingness to restore you? Why or why not?

  _____

  _____

  _____

  _____

- Under what conditions do you normally forgive someone? Is there any failure too great for you to forgive?

  _____

  _____

  _____

  _____

A Case Study

Imagine: He spent years in an epic battle with alcohol, losing his family and all of his friends except one: you. But through your encouragement, unwavering support, and tough love, his life is back on the right track. Relationships are being restored. He made a solemn vow to the Lord that he would never take another drink again, and he's shown you every reason to believe he'll keep it.

Late one Saturday night, you get a call from a bartender. Your friend gave the bartender the number because he couldn't dial it himself. He's too far under the influence and needs a ride home. So you do the duty of friendship and pick him up, help him into his apartment, and make sure he's asleep. Sometime late the next morning—or perhaps the afternoon—you and he will have to sit down together and face the facts. He's blown it. Big time.

- What would you say to your friend about all the ground he lost the night before? What would you do to help restore him?

- What would you tell him about God's perspective on his collapse—especially in light of his solemn vow?

- Why wasn't your friend's willpower—or Peter's, for that matter—enough to prevent a fall? Does God have another solution for our weaknesses other than his encouragement and our determination? If so, what?

Power

Almost seven weeks since the crucifixion, religious authorities are breathing a little more easily. The problem of Jesus has almost completely died down—there are still rumblings of sightings, but there isn't enough unrest to draw Rome's attention. The priests and scribes still have their jobs, most of the people seem to have come back to their senses, and the alleged Messiah is, in the eyes of most sane people, dead and gone.

Pilate too must be pleased at having avoided a nasty, full-blown revolt. It had been a dicey situation, and now the movers and shakers are reasonably content. The stability of his small territory has been maintained. The tension between Jew and Roman has returned to a live-and-let-live equilibrium again.

Pilate's only real problem now is his insomnia. His wife's warnings not to have anything to do with Yeshua keep ringing in his ears, even this long after the fact.

A handful of guards have a similar problem. Those who stood watch at Yeshua's tomb still have no idea what really happened that night. The rumble in the earth, the flash of light, the mysterious angel, the unsealed tomb—and no human activity in the garden cemetery. The next morning was chaotic, and they still can't understand why they weren't executed for failing to guard a simple tomb from theft—though some from their number were. But the bribe the others received for their self-incriminating lie—saying they were asleep when his disciples stole the body—wasn't as satisfying as it could have been. They sold a clear conscience and a decent night's sleep for much too low a price.

Meanwhile, the next of Jerusalem's feasts has arrived, and the disciples are gathered in an upper room praying. They are convinced they saw Yeshua ascend into heaven, and they are waiting for the power he promised. But what would it look like? Would they recognize the power when they saw it?

Inspired Words: Acts 2:1–40

Focus: Acts 2:1–14

On the streets below the room where the believers are gathered, Jerusalem is humming. Pilgrims from all parts of the world have made their way to the city for the Feast of Pentecost. The assembled believers have been diligently seeking God in prayer, as instructed by Jesus, and waiting to see what he promised. Suddenly, a roaring wind fills the house and tongues of fire fall on each person. The visitation is unmistakable. The promised power has arrived.

Peter is filled with words. In fact, each of the disciples has plenty to say, speaking the message of Jesus in other languages. The visitors in town for the feast hear the good news in their native tongue and are touched by the message and baffled by the messengers. Then Peter takes the lead. He stands up and

A NEW HARVEST

The Jewish Feast of Weeks was a one-day celebration that took place seven weeks after Passover—hence its other familiar names of *Shavuot* (Hebrew for "weeks") and Pentecost (from counting it as the fiftieth day after Passover). The primary focus of the Feast was the harvest. Offerings from the recent barley crop were brought in gratitude for what had already come, and firstfruit offerings of the upcoming wheat crop were brought in faith for what would be coming soon. It's no coincidence that God chose this harvest celebration as the occasion for the advent of the Holy Spirit. A harvest of disciples had already been gleaned from Jesus's ministry, and the firstfruits of a greater global harvest were offered when three thousand people turned to Jesus that day after Peter preached.

preaches the world's first post-ascension sermon. He steps into the role he will fill for the rest of his life: a vocal leader of the Jesus movement.

Discuss

- Peter's regrets and failures are nowhere evident in Acts 2. It's as though they never happened. He has "moved on" and gotten busy doing what God called him to do. Is anything from your past hindering your ability to be completely available to God? If so, how do you think God would want you to deal with it? Why is it so hard sometimes to move on?

  _____

  _____

  _____

  _____

35

Daring Faith: Acts 3:1–26

Focus: Acts 3:1–10

Peter and John encounter a familiar scene on their way to the temple to pray. A cripple is being carried to the gate so he can beg for alms from passers-by. But today is different than most other days. The disciples are filled with a boldness in faith that they never knew when Jesus was with them in the flesh. They look the man in the eyes and offer him something far better than silver or gold. Peter grabs his hand, pulls him to his feet before seeing any evidence of healing, and tells him to walk. Only then do the man's ankles and legs grow strong. He walks, jumps, and praises God vocally and visibly.

THE BEAUTIFUL GATE

The outer court of the Gentiles was open to anyone who revered the God of Israel, but the court of women was for Jews only, and the interior courts only got more exclusive. Between the court of Gentiles and the court of women stood a large, bronze-framed gate. It was the busiest gate into the temple, but only the ritually clean could pass through it—which meant the maimed and handicapped couldn't. This is where the lame man of Acts 3 was begging. It was, after all, the hour of afternoon prayer; there were plenty of people who would want to demonstrate their generous heart on their way into the presence of God. But the lame man healed by Peter and John received something greater than monetary support and something even greater than his health. He immediately received the right to enter further into the temple—which is why "he went with them *into the temple courts*, walking and jumping, and praising God" (Acts 3:8). He was now "clean" not only in the eyes of God but also in the eyes of the priests who would have prevented his worship inside.

36

It's a very public spectacle. People who have long passed this cripple, many of whom have even supported him with token offerings, are amazed at the sight. They are filled with wonder and awe, and Peter sees another opportunity. Again, he begins to preach.

Discuss

- People all around you are hurting physically, emotionally, and/or spiritually. How much of your reputation or your dignity would you be willing to risk to help them? How much faith do you have that your intervention can change their lives?

  _____

  _____

  _____

  _____

- Peter seized an opportunity to display the glory of Jesus. How diligently do you look for those kinds of opportunities? What is one act of faith you can do this week to help someone who's hurting?

  _____

  _____

  _____

  _____

Courageous Leadership: Acts 5:1–10

Many believers are selling their possessions, pooling their resources, and sharing with each other so no one would have any needs. It's a remarkable reflection of the love of Christ in their lives. Though the generosity isn't required of anyone, it's a natural response to the Spirit's presence. And it's being offered with complete transparency.

But there are always those who try to see how little they can get by with. In this case, it's a married couple named Ananias and Sapphira who feign greater generosity than they actually have. They have sold a piece of property and have told the church they are donating the full amount to the collective fund. Instead, they secretly keep a portion for themselves.

But there are no secrets with the Holy Spirit, and there is no room for a lack of integrity. The couple has lied to God, to Peter and the other leaders, and to the fellowship of believers.

The Spirit enables Peter to see through the charade. And unlike many later church leaders who would ignore the deception as a personal issue for Ananias and Sapphira to deal with, Peter confronts them. When he bluntly exposes Ananias's lie, the deceiver falls down dead. Later, his wife does the same when she is confronted. In these first days of the new creation, integrity seems to be a vital issue both to the Spirit and to Peter.

Discuss

- To what degree do you think the church today is known for its integrity? Do you think the Spirit does (or will) have as harsh a response to deception as he did with Ananias and Sapphira? Why or why not?

  _____

  _____

  _____

  _____

  _____

- How meticulous are you about your own integrity? Do you present yourself as more generous, loving, honest, etc., than you are? If so, why?

  _____

  _____

  _____

  _____

  _____

A CASE STUDY

Imagine: You're walking through the mall and see a quadriplegic in a wheelchair. Like most people, your normal reaction would be a non-reaction. But today, you feel a surge of boldness rising up within you. You walk over to the quadriplegic and the accompanying caretaker and ask if you can pray. Then you become even more assertive; you tell the person to stand up and walk.

- What attitudes or fears keep us from normally responding this way? Why do those hindrances tend to influence us more than Peter's example?
- Do you think the "surge of boldness" in this example is more likely to be the Holy Spirit or just wishful thinking? Why?
- How is Peter's bold ministry an example for us in less dramatic situations than a miraculous healing? In what other situations do you think we are called to confront evidence of the fall rather than ignore it?

39

Conflict

Josh grew up in a mostly Jewish neighborhood in New York, but a melting pot of cultures simmered only a couple of blocks away. Among his peers were Italian Catholics, American Protestants, Indian Hindus and Sikhs, Arab Muslims, Chinese and Vietnamese Buddhists, and, of course, a significant share of atheists and agnostics. Some adherents were extremely devout, others only nominal in their faith. Some were exclusive in their relationships, others very inclusive. And though cultural and religious differences boiled over every once in a while, everyone generally got along. They had to; they all had to share the same space.

Though everyone kept the peace most of the time, few people remained neutral. Josh came to a point in his life when he had to decide whether to continue the strict observance of Judaism that had been taught to him or taste a few other items on the religious buffet. And though his Jewish identity wouldn't

40

change at its core, he also found quite a few other voices to be rather compelling. His perspective was broadening and his understanding was being stretched. He would have to be both open and very discerning.

That's an appropriate attitude for any believer in any era. We have to be open to what God is doing but also discerning about what we encounter. The world is, and has always been, full of both truth and error. Learning the difference between them can often be a complicated process.

The Roman Empire was a complex melting pot of gods. The Roman pantheon, which overlapped extensively but not completely with Greek and Egyptian deities, was vast. And a common thread through all religious practice was emperor worship—the often-enforced veneration of the reigning Roman ruler. And, of

HOSPITALITY

In the ancient world, hospitality was an essential virtue, and a lack of hospitality was considered a blatant sin. This primarily grew out of the nomadic background of many Middle Eastern people as well as the inhospitable territory between towns. God's law given through Moses emphasized the importance of receiving strangers without favoritism. To offer food, water, and shelter to a traveler wasn't just nice; in some cases, it could be lifesaving.

There were unstated rules of hospitality for a visitor too. To refuse what a host put on the table was considered offensive and rude, a sign of contempt for the hospitality being offered. So Peter's visit to Cornelius, a Gentile from a non-kosher home, could have been a crisis of faith if God had not so emphatically directed him to go. In fact, he wouldn't have gone without such direct divine intervention. It was a major step for a Jew to enter an unclean household—and a highly controversial step in the eyes of observant Jews.

course, the Jewish faith that had been scattered across the empire was rooted in centuries of divine law and human tradition.

It was in this context that God chose to introduce his Son and birth his church among the nations. Confronting this fluid and sometimes volatile religious mix required strong leaders like Peter and Paul. God blessed them with strength, faith, revelation, and lots of grace—because sorting out the truth among so many competing beliefs would inevitably involve some mistakes and misjudgments. Peter, well familiar with those sorts of stumbles, would play a key role.

A Course Correction: Acts 10:1–11:18

Focus: Acts 10:1–19, 44–48

Peter will later be known as the apostle to the Jews, while Paul will become famous as the apostle to the Gentiles. But it's Peter through whom God first chooses to swing open the door of salvation to non-Jews. His vision on a rooftop shifts the paradigm of the early church and gives it a straight path into the Greco-Roman world.

Cornelius is a man of considerable means, power, and authority. As a centurion, he is in charge of a fighting force of one hundred Roman soldiers. He is also what the Jews call a God-fearer, a Gentile who has accepted the Jewish God and faith as his own but has stopped short of adopting the practices—circumcision and dietary laws, for example—necessary to become a Jewish proselyte.

In divinely coordinated timing, God gives Cornelius and Peter complementary visions. He tells Cornelius to send men to bring Peter to his house, and he shows Peter that keeping one's distance from Gentiles for dietary and other reasons is no longer necessary—nor, as the church will find out, even feasible or pos-

THE GENTILE QUESTION

Long before Jesus and the early church, most Jews believed Gentiles could be saved by converting to Judaism. Some also believed in Gentile salvation through faith in the God of Israel and adherence to the seven laws traditionally said to have been given to Noah (against idolatry and sexual immorality, among others). Though many Jews thought this standard was much too low, the testimony of the Holy Spirit himself opened up the gates into the kingdom even wider. Astonishingly, the Spirit came upon people who simply believed.

sible. Why? Because salvation is offered to Gentiles too, and the church will generate many gatherings in which Jews and Gentiles fellowship together, work alongside each other, and even eat together. They must do so without one member considering the other unclean. No walls could separate Jews and Gentiles, slave or free, male or female. The body of Christ would be a united whole.

At Cornelius's house, Peter explains the gospel to a large gathering. As he is speaking, the Spirit falls on everyone present. It's astonishing and indisputable evidence that God is making no distinction between Jew and Gentile. The only reasonable response is praise.

Discuss

- How would you respond if God told you to do something that would violate one of your long-held personal values?

  _____

  _____

  _____

  _____

- If the Spirit dramatically manifested himself among people who had never been to church or read the Bible, would you be more likely to feel jealous or praise God? Why?

_____

_____

_____

_____

_____

A Council: Acts 15:1–35

Focus: Acts 15:1–21

Some Pharisees who had become Christians were finding the Gentile mission very difficult to reconcile with Scripture. After all, it was clear in the Spirit-inspired law of Moses that circumcision was to be a sign of the people of God (Exod. 12:48–49; Lev. 12:3). In fact, all of the laws of Torah were to be a sign that set God's people apart from the world. And it simply isn't possible for the Spirit to contradict himself. Therefore, Gentiles who accept the Jewish Messiah should be circumcised and observe the Torah.

The answer—that salvation is by grace through faith alone, and neither circumcision nor any other work is a prerequisite of grace—is hard for them to see. So a council of church leaders convenes in Jerusalem to settle the issue. Jew and Gentile believers, apostles, and elders offer their views. After "much discussion," Peter stands up and lays out his simple, evidence-based argument: "God, who knows the heart, showed that he accepted them by giving the Holy Spirit to them, just as he did to us. He made no distinction between us and them, for he purified their hearts by faith" (15:8–9). In other words, if the Spirit isn't keeping his distance from uncircumcised Gentiles, why should we?

In the end, James, the leader of the Jerusalem church, agrees. The council strongly urges Gentiles to reject the rituals of paganism—meat sacrificed to idols and rites of sexual immorality—as incompatible with their new faith. An unstated but vital assumption is that the Holy Spirit will conform Gentile believers to the image of Christ and the character of God, bringing them in line with the other, non-Israel-specific commandments. This new freedom is no license for sin. But the liberty to believe and worship and be filled with the Spirit apart from Jewish rites becomes official church policy.

Discuss

- How difficult do you think it was for Peter to advocate for Gentiles among his Jewish brothers? How difficult do you think it might have been for him to endorse the ministry of Paul, who was once an enemy of the disciples?

  _____

  _____

  _____

  _____

  _____

- How well do you think Christians today affirm ministries that employ unfamiliar methods? Why?

  _____

  _____

  _____

  _____

  _____

A Confrontation: Galatians 2:1–21

Focus: Galatians 2:11–21

Peter's resolve on the issue of accommodating Gentile believers has wavered since the Jerusalem meeting. He has been accepting invitations to dine with Greek friends in Antioch, but when some disciples of James visit, he begins to distance himself from the Gentile believers in order to appease the Jewish believers.

The change in Peter's behavior is noticeable. The bold apostle has suddenly allowed the pressure of Jewish observers to intimidate him. Even Barnabas, Paul's companion, joins in this "hypocrisy" (2:13). It has become a public issue, so Paul confronts Peter publicly. And there's no evidence in the New Testament that Peter ever rejected the criticism. In his maturity, he has become correctable.

Discuss

- How do we know where to draw the line between the absolutes of our faith and the freedom we're given in Christ? When is it right to confront others who may be abusing their freedom in Christ?

  _____

  _____

  _____

  _____

- Paul was adamant that Peter shouldn't avoid eating with Gentiles just to appease Jewish believers. However, he also taught that we shouldn't use our freedom to offend others (Rom. 14:19–20; 1 Cor. 10:31–33). Why do you think Paul was less concerned about offending strict Jewish Christians in this particular case?

_____

_____

_____

_____

A Case Study

Imagine: You've grown up in a very conservative Christian sect that discourages all forms of interaction with the secular world except the most unavoidable. But a new faction within your community has recently begun preaching a new interpretation of the sect's principles, saying that the only way to impact the world is to mix and mingle with it—to get involved in secular organizations and to try to understand secular culture, including its media and entertainment and ideologies. Needless to say, there's quite a conflict between the traditional faction and the progressive one. And your concept of holiness is being stretched beyond your comfort level.

- Why is change, especially in matters of faith, so controversial and contested?
- How is it possible to know when a new direction is initiated by God and when it isn't? How do we balance our faithfulness to long-held values with our willingness to be moved by God's Spirit?
- What was Paul's answer to this tension between old and new perspectives? What was Peter's?

Faithfulness

1–2 PETER

Romans didn't understand Christians. Upon hearing the terminology of the Lord's Supper—"brothers and sisters" who commune at "love feasts," eating the body and blood of their Lord—many called the cult incestuous and cannibalistic. They also didn't understand why followers of an executed prophet wouldn't also be able to worship the Roman gods and emperors. As deniers of the emperor's deity, Christians were considered "atheists." Their defiance of Rome's religious culture would, it was feared, undermine society by provoking the gods' wrath. As a result, the first century was marked with seasons of active and growing resentment toward Christians.

This was particularly acute in Rome in the AD 60s when Nero ruled. In AD 64, a large section of Rome burned, and

JESUS FISH

Just as many do today in oppressive countries, early believers lived in imminent danger of persecution at various times by either Romans or Jews. The symbol of the fish seems to have been a common way for Christians to secretly identify each other without endangering themselves. When meeting someone who might be a believer—but, in fact, might not—a Christian would use a stick or a toe to casually draw one arc of the simple fish figure on the ground—an innocent doodle if the other party didn't recognize it. If the other person was also a Christian, he or she would complete the symbol with the other arc. The two would then be free to talk openly with each other about their faith.

rumors began to surface that the emperor had started the fires in order to confiscate the land for his own building projects. To counter these rumors, Nero blamed Christians for the fire. Christian-killing became an acceptable and popular indulgence. The emperor himself would sometimes douse believers in tar and set them on fire to be human torches lighting his gardens. Some Christians were sewn into the skins of animals and fed to starving dogs while evil mobs cheered. Others were nailed to crosses. It was during this persecution in Rome that Paul most likely lost his life. Peter followed soon after.

This persecution is the context in which Peter wrote his two letters to Christians scattered across Asia Minor (modern Turkey). The purpose of the first letter was to explain the Christian way of living in exile, especially in an oppressive situation. The second letter warned against the many variations on the gospel and urged believers to cling to the truths they had been taught.

Far From Home: 1 Peter

Focus: 1 Peter 4:12–19

Peter's first letter is filled with words of encouragement and promises of strength and hope and glory:

"An inheritance that can never perish" (1:4). "Set your hope fully on the grace to be given you when Jesus Christ is revealed" (1:13). "Born again, not of perishable seed, but of imperishable" (1:23). "A chosen people, a royal priesthood, a holy nation, a people belonging to God" (2:9). "Live such good lives among the pagans . . ." (2:12). "Christ suffered for you, leaving you an

EARLY CHRISTIAN HERESIES

False teachings about the person and work of Jesus began to spring up very early in the history of the church. None had highly developed doctrines until the second century, but Peter and the other apostles who knew Jesus well frequently had to confront the seeds of deception. Among those heresies that eventually formed among Christians were:

Gnosticism—Gnostics believed that salvation comes through special, exclusive, highly guarded knowledge of spiritual things. They often functioned in secret societies and emphasized the purity of spiritual things and the corruption of all matter. Variations on Gnosticism are still widely believed today.

Docetism—From the Greek *dokesis,* "to seem," Docetists claimed that Jesus was not a real human being and that he only appeared to have a human body.

Ebionism—Ebionites believed that Jesus was fully human but not divine. He somehow managed to perfectly obey the law of Moses, and as a result, God rewarded him by making him the Messiah.

Arianism—Arians denied the Trinity. They saw Jesus as a special creation of God, and even a demigod, but certainly something less than God himself.

example" (2:21). "Do not repay evil with evil" (3:9). "Even if you should suffer for what is right, you are blessed" (3:14). "Since Christ suffered in his body, arm yourselves also with the same attitude" (4:1). "Do not be surprised at the painful trial you are suffering" (4:12). "Cast all your anxiety on him because he cares for you" (5:7).

These words are profound in any season of life. During an intense crisis, however, they are life-giving truths. And, according to Peter, there's even a hidden benefit in a believer's suffering: it refines faith and proves its authenticity. Pretenders and compromisers don't bear up under persecution. True believers do. Those who count the cost and follow Jesus anyway can know that they are truly his friends.

Peter will live up to his words. Around AD 64 or 65, he will be executed for his faith in Jesus, and he'll make a major statement when he does. According to tradition, he will ask to be crucified upside down because he feels unworthy to die in the same manner as his Lord.

Discuss

- What sorts of ambitions or fears might keep someone from living an uncompromising life of faith in Jesus? In what ways have you experienced temptations to compromise?

_____

_____

_____

_____

_____

_____

_____

Trained in Truth: 2 Peter

Focus: 2 Peter 1:16–21

His magnetic personality and decisive message drew quite a following, first in Indiana, then in California, and finally in South America. But what began as a movement ended as a deadly cult, as more than nine hundred people drank poison at his command and died. In his followers' minds, this would be their salvation. In the eyes of God, it was a horrific tragedy of deception.

The familiar story of Jim Jones and The People's Temple is an extreme case of devastating doctrine, but it's also a graphic picture of more subtle deceptions. All heresy is a poisonous drink that can lead to death. And because the lies appear as truth and the darkness comes as an angel of light, a passive approach doesn't work. Guarding against deception needs to be an intentional effort.

Peter's second epistle is a warning against heresy, and it has harsh words about the false teachers who infiltrate God's people and lead them astray. The truth of God will always focus on the power and coming of Jesus, on his majestic glory, and be rooted in prophecy and the rest of Scripture.

Why is this so important? Because an end is coming, both for an individual's life in this age and for the entire creation as we know it. When Jesus comes again, lies will be exposed. And those who have wielded them against God's people, as well as the people who believed them, will be held accountable.

Discuss

- What are some ways to know when you are being spiritually deceived? In what ways might God guide us in order to keep us within his truth?

_____

_____

_____

_____

- In your opinion, what false teachings are the greatest threat to the church today?

_____

_____

_____

_____

A Case Study

Imagine: You live in a country where Christians are only two percent of the population, and the only government-sanctioned religion regards Jesus as nothing more than a good teacher. The official national policy has always been complete religious freedom, but the law isn't enforced very well. Those who oppress Christians are never reprimanded. As a result, Christian businesses suffer from unfair taxes and a lack of patrons; Christian children don't get into good schools, even with excellent grades; whenever there's a conflict between a Christian and a non-Christian, the courts usually favor the non-Christian; believers are systematically excluded from politics and public discourse; and media portrayals of Christians mock the faith relentlessly.

- Do you think it would be possible to change the public's perception of Christians? If so, how? What could you personally do to change the image?
- To what extent would you legally challenge anti-Christian injustice? How vocally would you protest? Do you think your reactions would enhance or undermine the public's perception of Christians?
- What truths from 1 Peter might help someone handle this kind of situation?

Conclusion

Jesus gazed into Peter's eyes, deep into his soul, and saw what Peter could one day be: a loyal friend and one of the most prominent leaders of the church.

Jesus probably smiled at the enthusiasm of this follower. Not even a lake full of water would stop him from reaching out to his Master. At Jesus's command, Peter would step out onto the water and walk. And when Jesus said that he must wash Peter's feet in order for the disciple to continue his relationship with him, Peter would ask Jesus to wash not just his feet but his head and his hands as well. Peter always wanted more.

Peter was a trustworthy friend. When God wanted to show Gentiles his offer of salvation, he entrusted the vision to Peter first. Peter was willing to attend to the everyday details of life with the same faithfulness with which he climbed mountains to see Jesus. He provided valuable leadership that the fledgling church desperately needed. Knowing his time on earth was drawing to a close, he penned letters of encouragement and instruction.

Peter wasn't perfect, but he was always trying, always moving forward, always willing to proceed. He's an example of what it means to live a daring, all-out life for the Lord.

How much did Peter love Jesus? Enough to follow him to the cross to die in his service. And how much did Jesus love Peter? Enough to be unwaveringly patient, enough to call an erratic disciple a rock, enough to train him as a mighty soldier and a treasured companion. And that's the good news; because the Lord found this very human hero endearing, there's hope for all of us. Peter was Jesus's friend—and so are you.

Leader's Notes

Session 1

John 1:35–42, second discussion question. This doesn't have to lead to a discussion of major, life-changing implications—although it might. Let the conversation go there if it will, but there's no need to push it in that direction. Wrestling with the call of Jesus in a more immediate but relatively minor aspect of daily life may be more relevant to participants and can have significant impact.

Session 2

A Case Study. Group members may have a strong opinion of the right thing to do in this situation, but help them see that Scripture itself isn't exactly clear on the issue. In many instances, early Christians were very vocal about their faith in spite of persecution (see Peter's comment in Acts 4:19–20, for example). On the other hand, during periods of severe oppression from rulers or the culture at large, Christians often lived relatively quiet lives and met for worship covertly (see Peter's instructions in 1 Peter 3:15, for example, in which he urges believers to defend their faith gently, and even then only when asked). This tension has always been present in times of persecution.

Session 3

Peter's vow of loyalty to live and die with Jesus and his later disavowal may not seem to us to be quite as serious a sin as the Bible makes it out to be because, in our culture, words are thrown around pretty casually. But in a largely oral culture, vows were as binding as a written and signed legal contract is today. Peter's promise to stick with Jesus might as well have been engraved in stone—and so might his denial. This verbal contradiction was a serious conundrum for him. And the grace he received for it later was much more than a casual "don't worry about it, it's over." It was a complete erasure of very concrete statements.

Session 4

Acts 2:1–40. The word that sets up Peter's speech in Acts 2:14—translated variously as "addressed" or "declared" to them—is actually a strong expression that literally emphasizes the enthusiasm of the speaker. Again, Peter's zeal shows through—this time fueled by the zeal of the indwelling Spirit.

Session 5

Acts 2, first discussion question. At some point in the discussion, help participants see their failures from God's perspective. You may want to ask a question that reveals how irrational our regrets can be. For example: "Do you think God prefers for us to dwell on our failures or to move past them?" Any good father, especially God, would want regrets left behind, both for his love and for practical reasons.

Session 6

Acts 10:1–11:18, second discussion question. The hypothetical statement about the Holy Spirit making himself manifest to people who had never read the Bible doesn't exactly parallel Cornelius's situation. He was, after all, a God-fearer. But it serves as a somewhat accurate example of how odd the Spirit coming upon Gentiles would look to first-century Jews. In fact, it would have seemed even more absurd to them than the Spirit spontaneously falling, for example, upon the most stridently agnostic faculty members of a secular, liberal university would seem to us.

Acts 15, second discussion question. If possible, help keep the discussion focused on ministries with outside-the-box methodology, not those with doctrine that clearly violates biblical orthodoxy. Christians are right to reject the latter.

Galatians 2, second discussion question. Paul's approach to this issue is complicated. He rebuked Peter for appeasing the legalists, but he also had Timothy circumcised so as not to offend Jews on their mission trips (see Acts 16:1–3). The explanation for such seeming contradiction may lie in the fact that Paul wanted to avoid all kinds of unnecessary offense, and in Peter's behavior in Antioch, Gentile believers who were new to the faith were already being offended. So the issue there wasn't a simply matter of avoiding offense, it was a matter of which party to offend. And, as always, Paul's solution leaned toward the side of freedom and grace.

A Case Study. Some relevant passages might include: 1 Peter 1:6–7; 2:11–17; 3:8–16; 4:12–19; and 5:8–11.

Bibliography

Alexander, David, and Pat Alexander. *Zondervan Handbook to the Bible*. Grand Rapids: Zondervan, 1999.

Arnold, Clinton E. *Zondervan Illustrated Bible Backgrounds Commentary*. Grand Rapids: Zondervan, 2002.

Card, Michael. *A Fragile Stone*. Downers Grove, IL: InterVarsity Press, 2003.

Chilton, Bruce, et al. *The Cambridge Companion to the Bible*. Cambridge and New York: Cambridge University Press, 1997.

Flynn, Leslie B. *From Clay to Rock: Personal Insights into Life from Simon Peter*. Chappaqua, NY: Christian Herald Books, 1981.

Geisler, Norman. *A Popular Survey of the New Testament*. Grand Rapids: Baker Books, 2007.

Gower, Ralph. *The New Manners and Customs of Bible Times*. Chicago: Moody, 2005.

Kaiser, Walter C., Jr., and Duane Garrett, eds. *Archaeological Study Bible*. Grand Rapids: Zondervan, 2006.

Keener, Craig S. *The IVP Bible Background Commentary: New Testament*. Downers Grove, IL: InterVarsity Press, 1993.

Powell, Ivor. *Simon Peter: Fisherman from Galilee*. Grand Rapids: Kregel, 1996.

Walk Thru the Bible. *The Daily Walk Bible.* Carol Stream, IL: Tyndale, 2007.

Walker, Scott. *Footsteps of the Fisherman.* Minneapolis: Augsburg Fortress, 2003.

Wagner, C. Peter. *The Book of Acts: A Commentary.* Ventura, CA: Regal Books, 2008.

Witherington, Ben, III. *New Testament History: A Narrative Account.* Grand Rapids: Baker Academic, 2001.

WALK THRU THE BIBLE®

Helping people everywhere
live God's Word

For more than three decades, Walk Thru the Bible has created discipleship materials and cultivated leadership networks that together are reaching millions of people through live seminars, print publications, audiovisual curricula, and the Internet. Known for innovative methods and high-quality resources, we serve the whole body of Christ across denominational, cultural, and national lines. Through our strong and cooperative international partnerships, we are strategically positioned to address the church's greatest need: developing mature, committed, and spiritually reproducing believers.

Walk Thru the Bible communicates the truths of God's Word in a way that makes the Bible readily accessible to anyone. We are committed to developing user-friendly resources that are Bible centered, of excellent quality, life changing for individuals, and catalytic for churches, ministries, and movements; and we are committed to maintaining our global reach through strategic partnerships while adhering to the highest levels of integrity in all we do.

Walk Thru the Bible partners with the local church worldwide to fulfill its mission, helping people "walk thru" the Bible with greater clarity and understanding. Live seminars and small group curricula are taught in over 45 languages by more than 80,000 people in more than 70 countries, and more than 100 million devotionals have been packaged into daily magazines, books, and other publications that reach over five million people each year.

Walk Thru the Bible
4201 North Peachtree Road
Atlanta, GA 30341-1207
770-458-9300
www.walkthru.org

Read the entire Bible in one year, thanks to the systematic reading plan in the best-selling **Daily Walk** *devotional.*

The ***Daily Walk*** devotional magazine includes book introductions, charts outlining book and chapter themes, and background information on each day's reading. Insightful observations shed light on the culture, the history, and the context of passages. Each daily reading is loaded with helpful applications that enable you to apply biblical truth to your life. Readers are sure to find the time they spend in the Bible more productive and rewarding than ever before.

Ideal for church-wide or group Bible study, bulk subscriptions to ***Daily Walk*** offering significant savings can be purchased online at www.walkthru.org. Discounted individual subscriptions are also available online.

WALK THRU THE BIBLE

www.walkthru.org

Individual Orders: **800-877-5539**   Bulk Orders: **800-998-0814**